ADVENTURE

For the Early Intermediate Piano Student

Unlock the Magic: A Piano Adventure Awaits!

Step into a world of enchantment and adventure with an Adventure Solos collection entitled "A Magical Forest Quest"—a spellbinding piano solo story progression for the intermediate piano student. Inspired by the magical allure and timeless intrigue of ancient and modern fairy tales alike, this book invites you on a musical quest through a forest teeming with wonder and peril.

Encounter dangerous patrol guards along the mountainside, dangerous riders, and secret messages hidden in the shadows. This collection is sure to delight pianists of all ages as you navigate your way through shimmering glades, moonlit clearings, and shadowy groves. Each piece is a chapter in your own journey, brimming with soaring melodies, mysterious harmonies, and thrilling twists. Dare to enter the Ethereal Glade of Mischief, outsmart the pursuant in the Rider's Resolve, dance the Impish Reel, and discover the secrets of Perilous Skies.

Perfect for intermediate pianists, these pieces balance lyrical beauty with moments of daring excitement, providing challenges that are as rewarding to play as they are to hear. Each piece is crafted to transport you—and your audience—into a world of magic, danger, and wonder.

Will you complete the journey and unlock the secrets of the Magical Forest Quest? Your odyssey begins with your first note. Let the magic guide your hands.

Copyright © 2024 by Elizabeth Bucura
ISBN 9798301372537
Independently Published

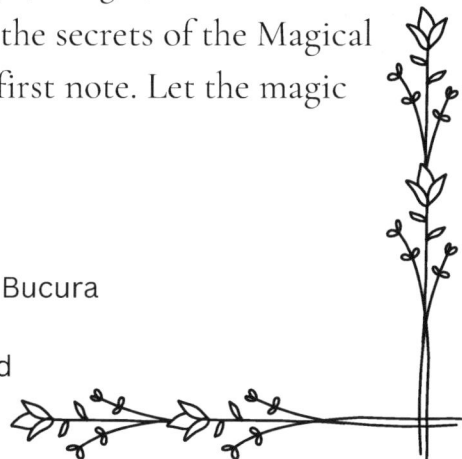

ADVENTURE SOLOS

For the Early Intermediate Piano Student

A MAGICAL FOREST QUEST

Magestic Lull

Elizabeth Bucura

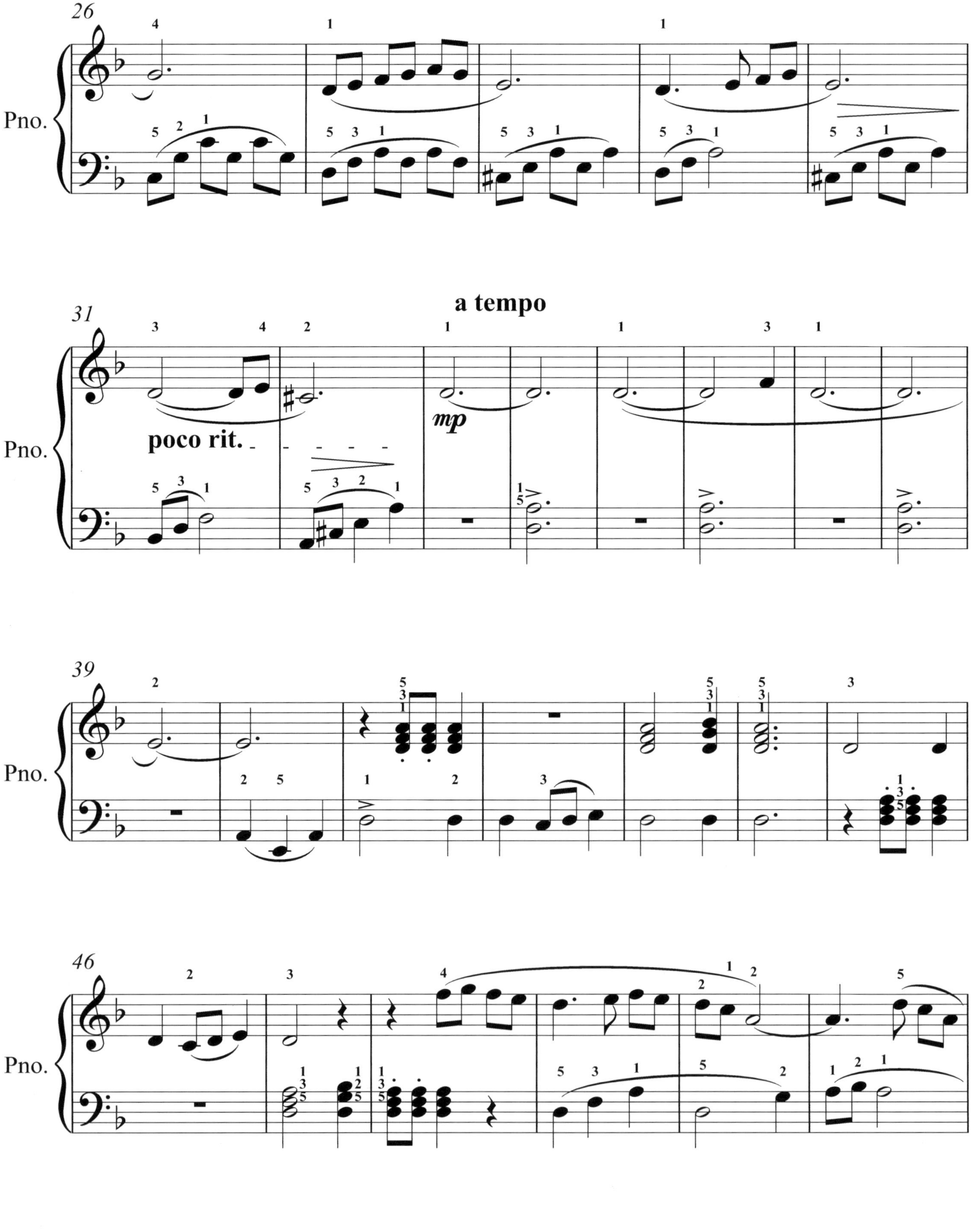
26
Pno.
31
a tempo
Pno.
poco rit.
mp
39
Pno.
46
Pno.

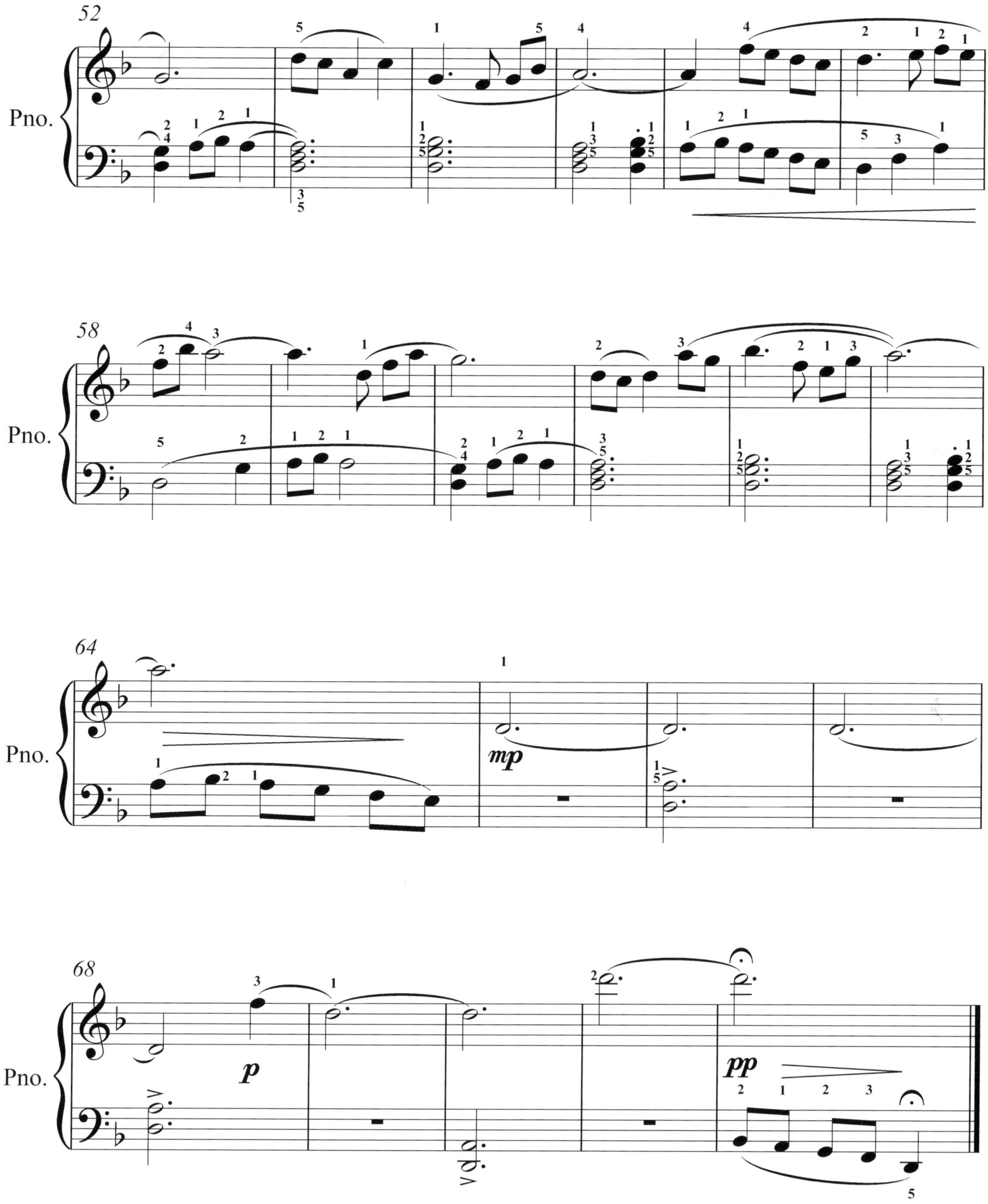
52
Pno.
58
Pno.
64
Pno.
mp
68
Pno.
p
pp

Perilous Skies

Elizabeth Bucura

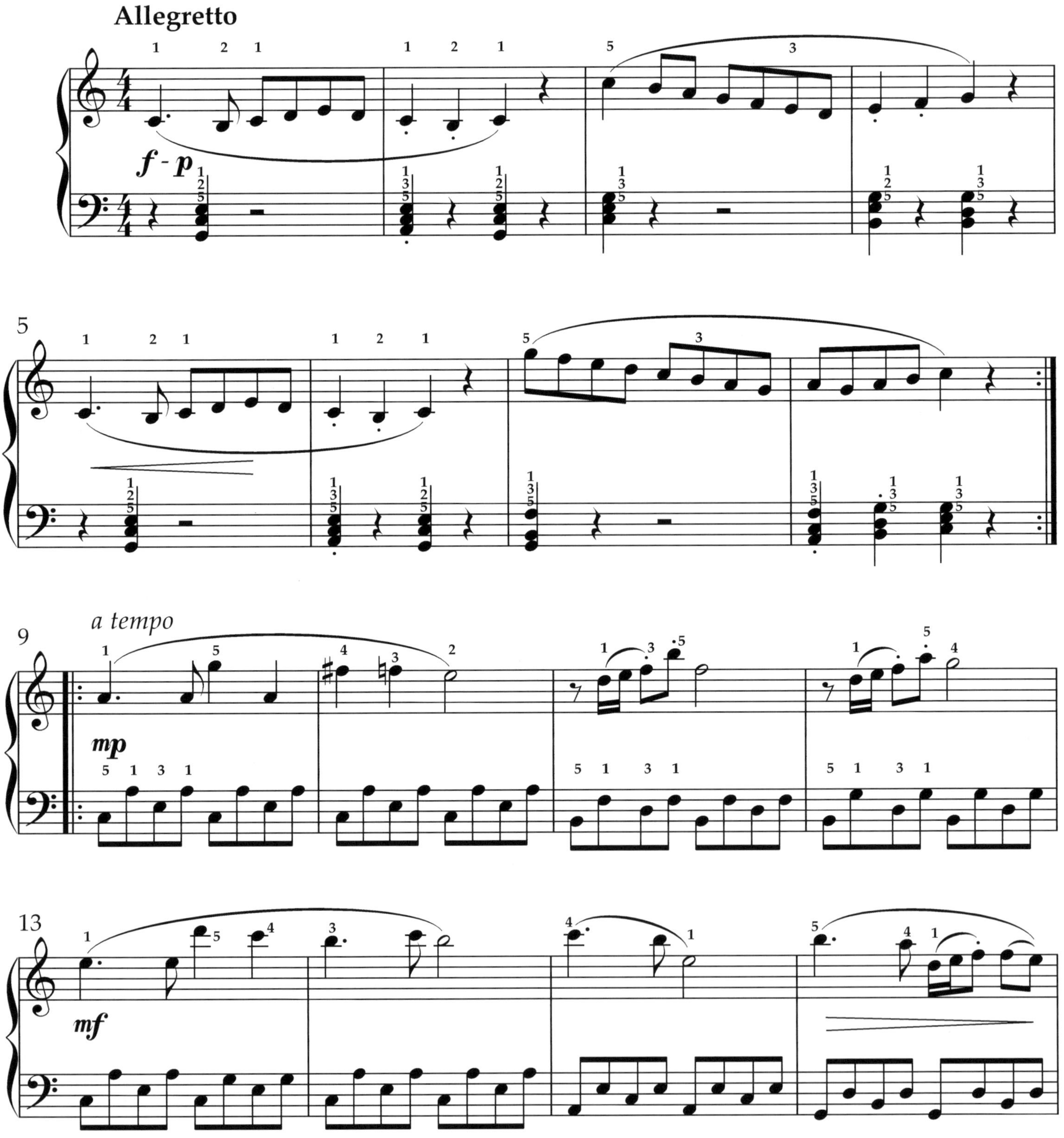

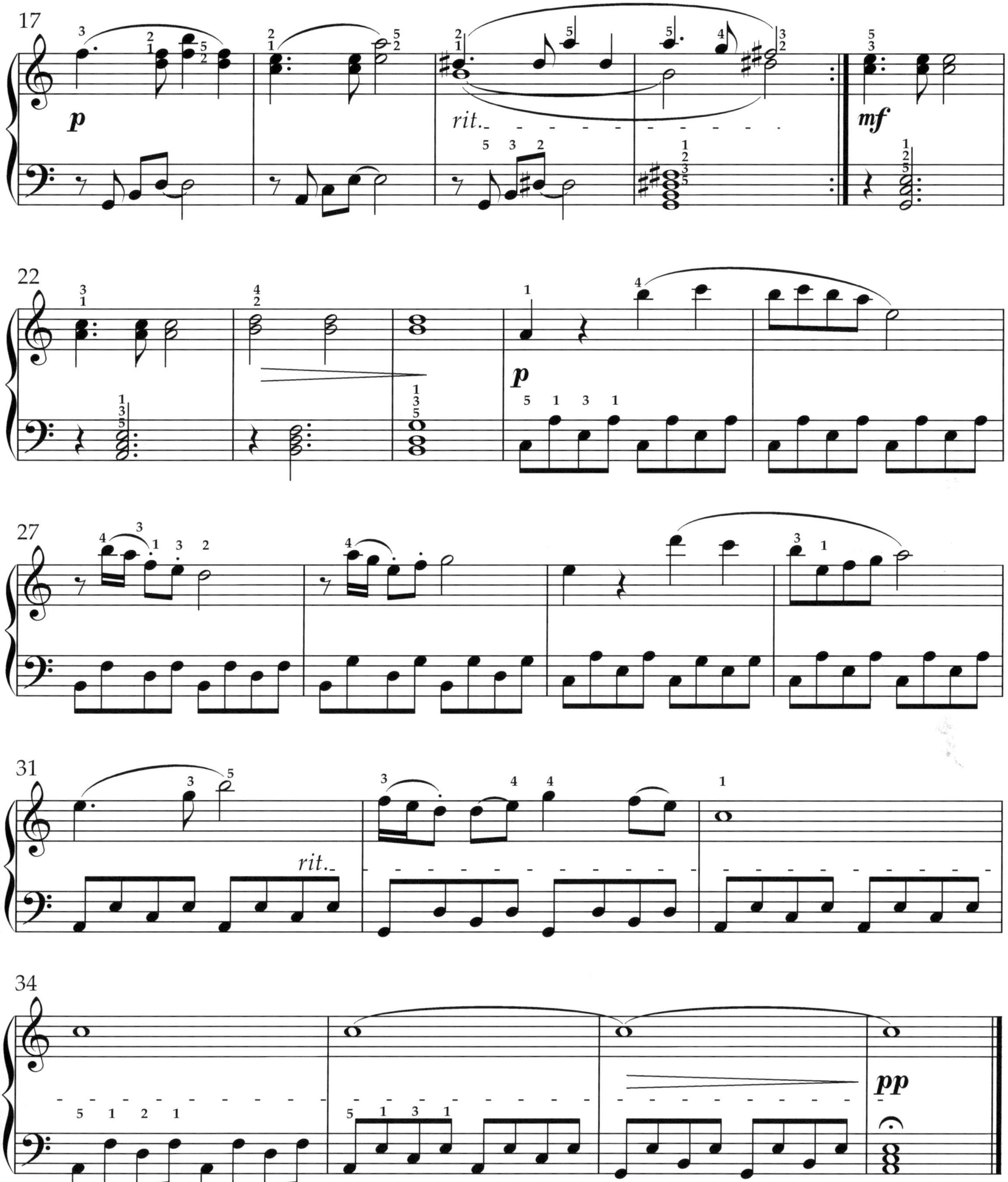
p
rit.
mf
p
rit.
pp

Enchanted Quest of the Brave Heart

Elizabeth Bucura

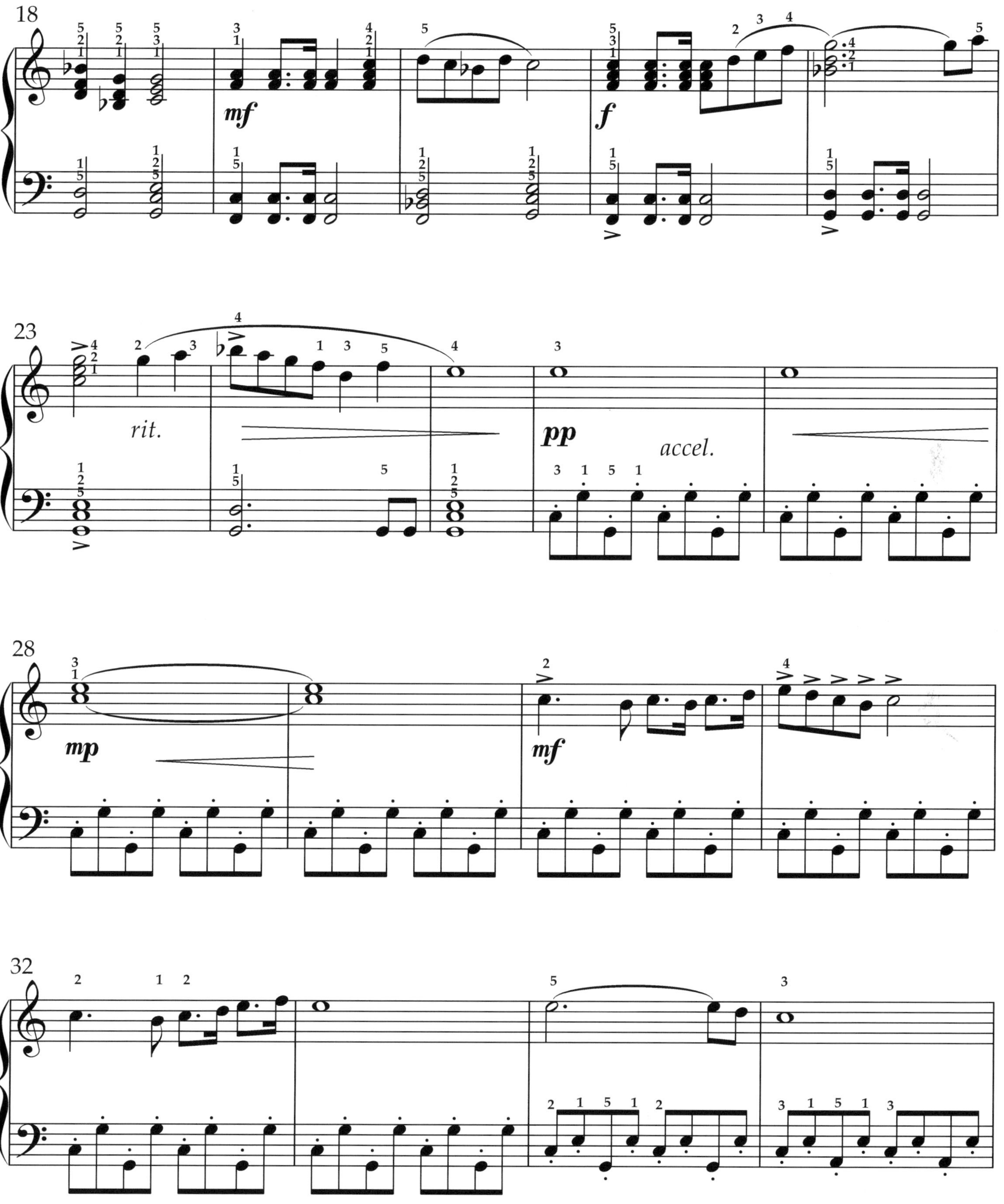
18
mf
f
23
rit.
pp
accel.
28
mp
mf
32

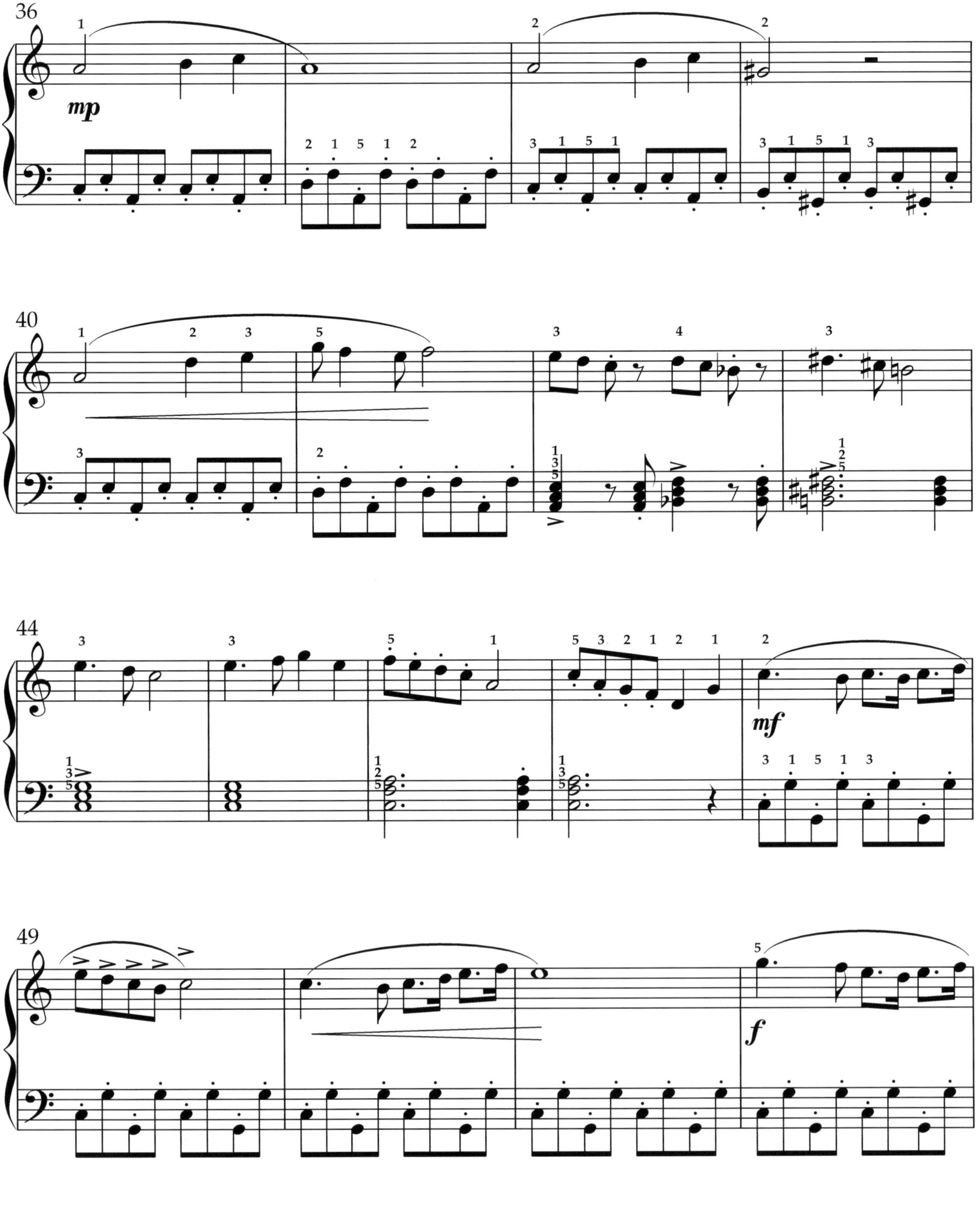
36
mp
40
44
mf
49
f

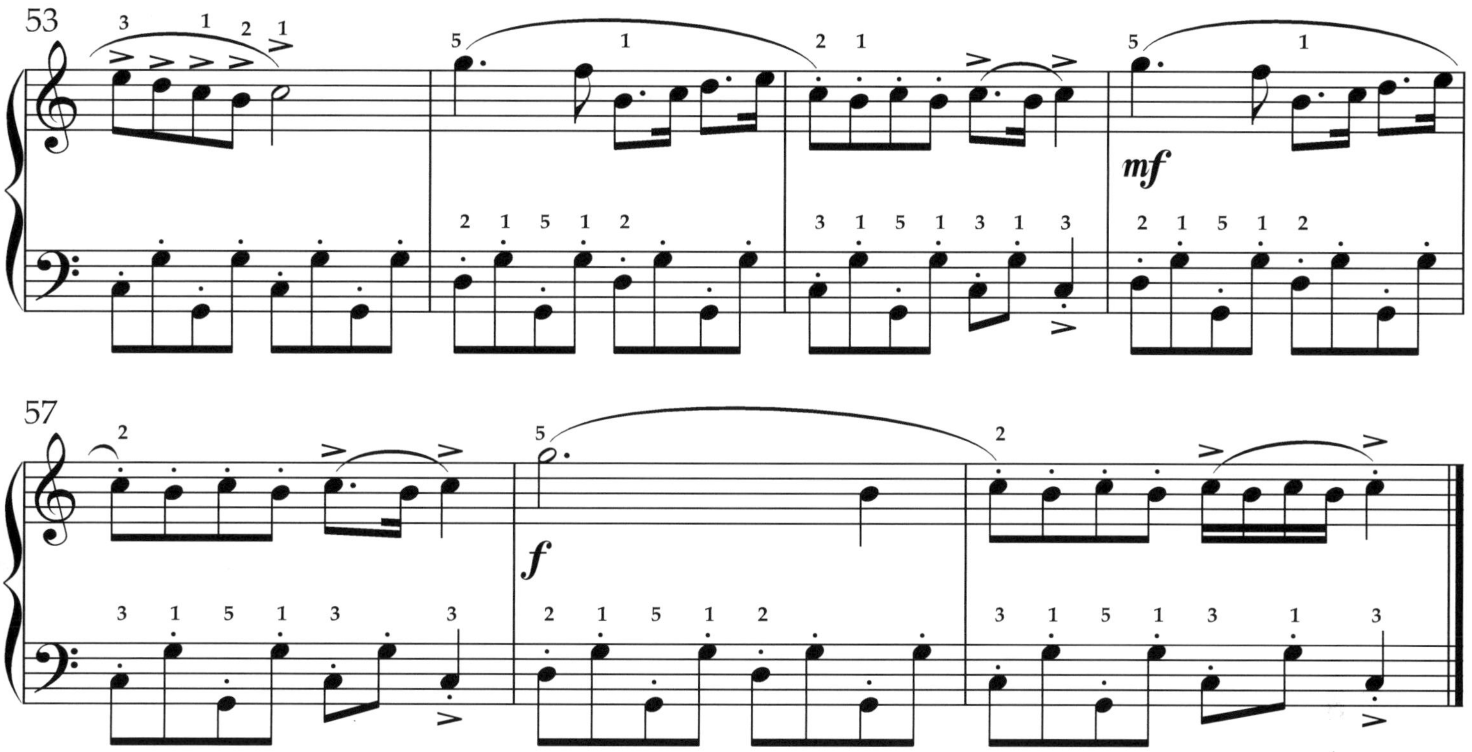
53
mf
57
f

Mountainside Patrol

Elizabeth Bucura

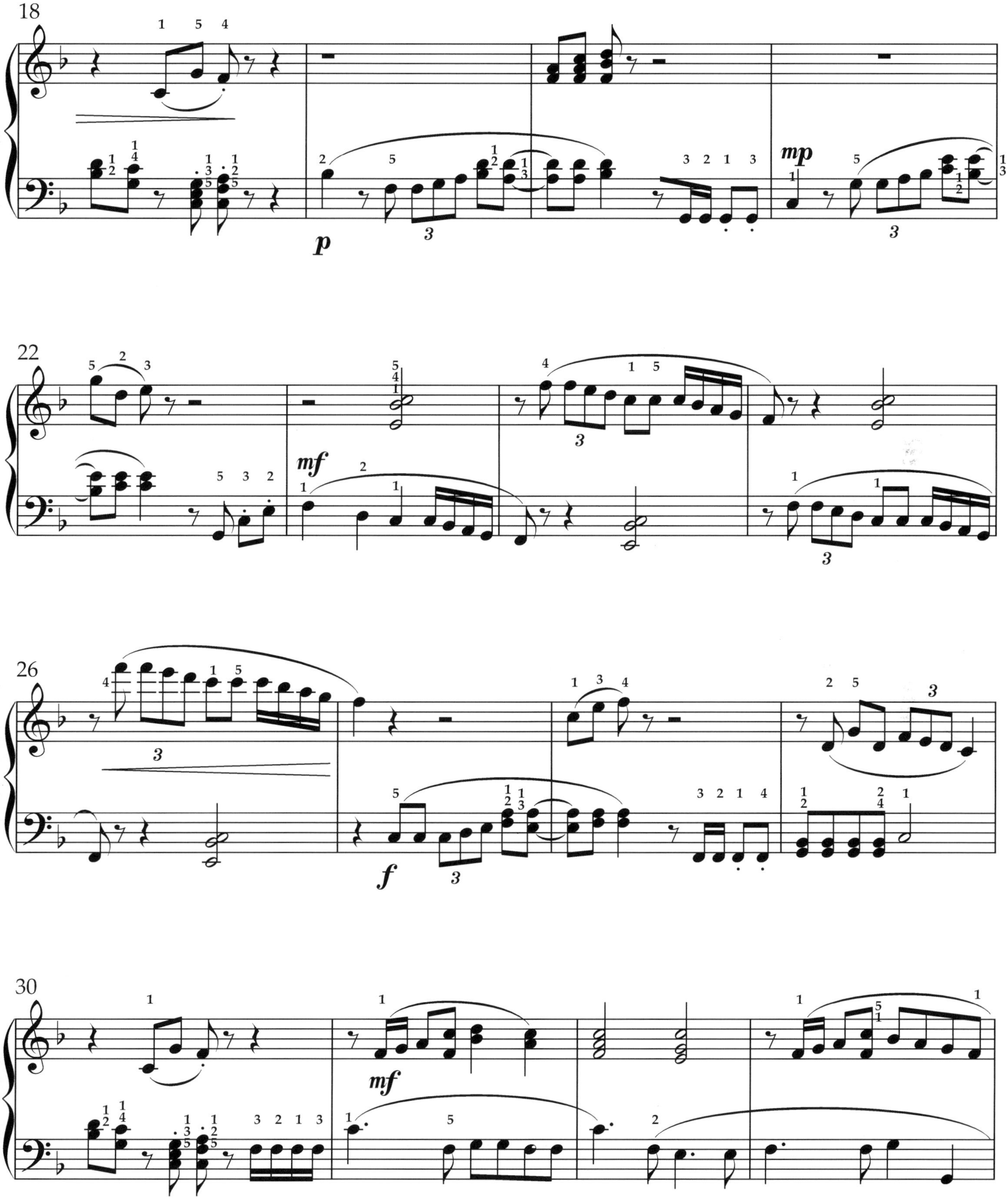
18
p
mp
22
mf
26
f
30
mf

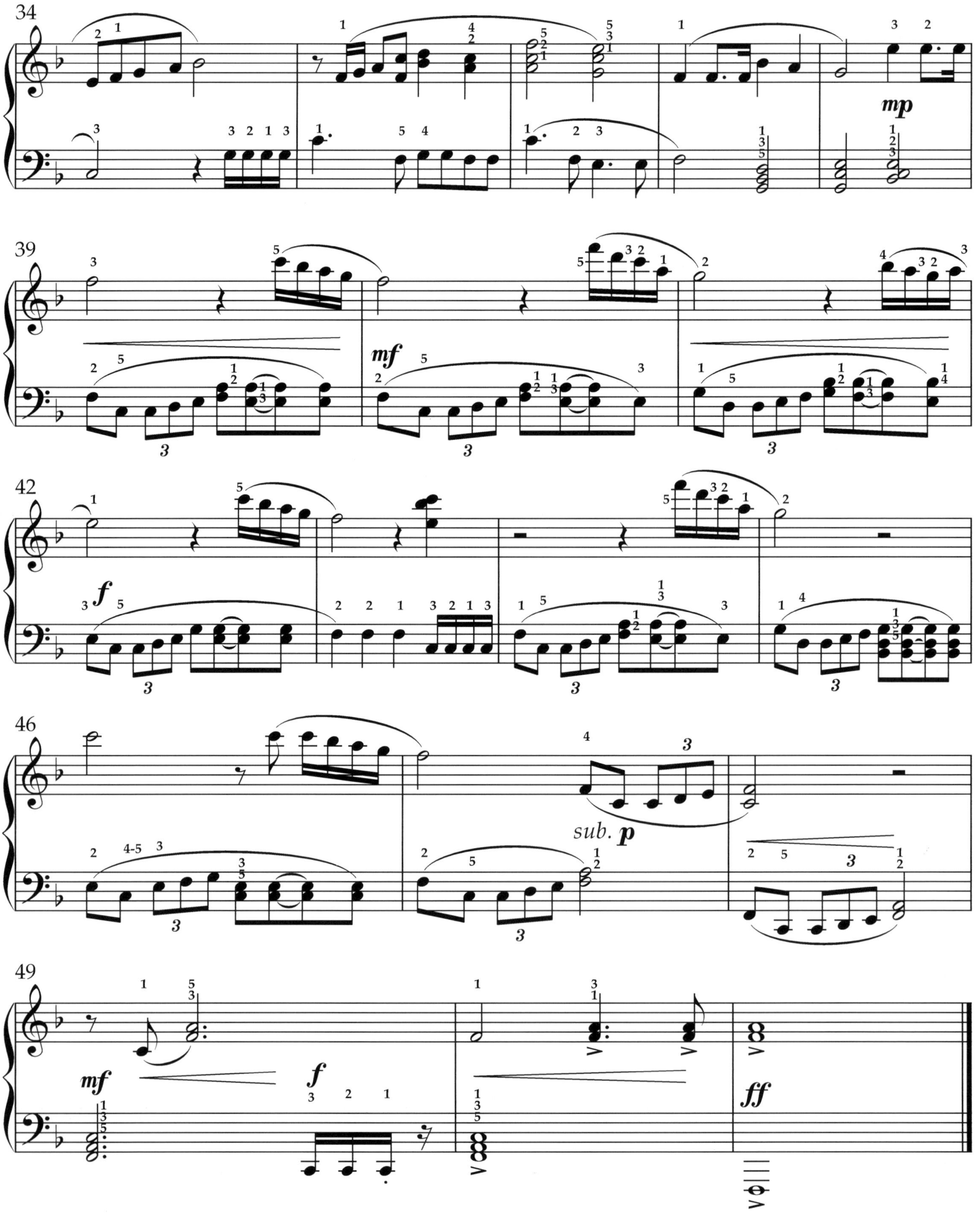
34
mp
39
mf
42
f
46
sub. p
49
mf
f
ff

The Rider's Resolve

Elizabeth Bucura

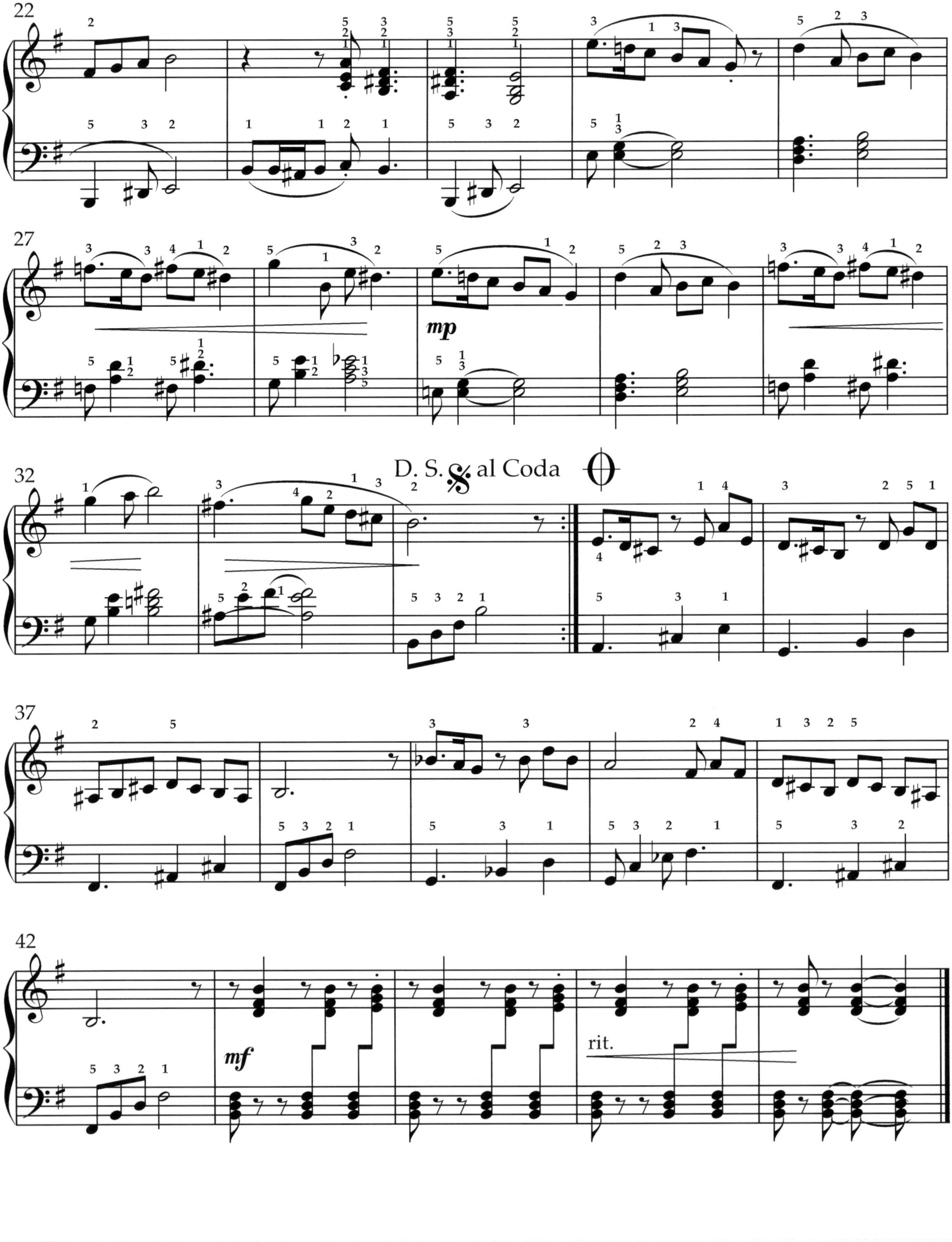
22
27
mp
32
D. S. al Coda
37
42
mf
rit.

Message in the Shadows

Elizabeth Bucura

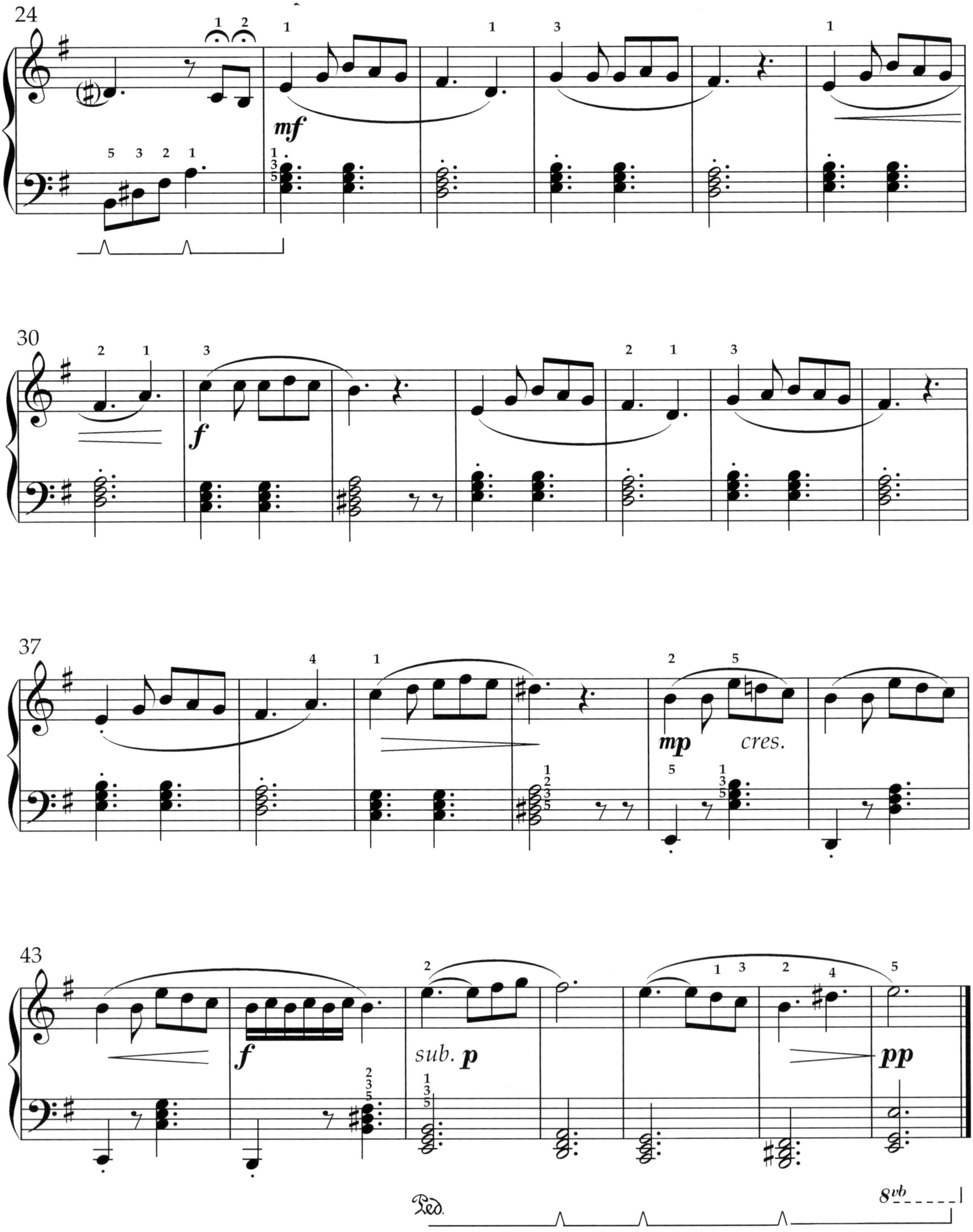
24
mf
30
f
37
mp
cres.
43
f
sub. p
pp
Ped.
8vb

Ethereal Glade of Mischief

Elizabeth Bucura

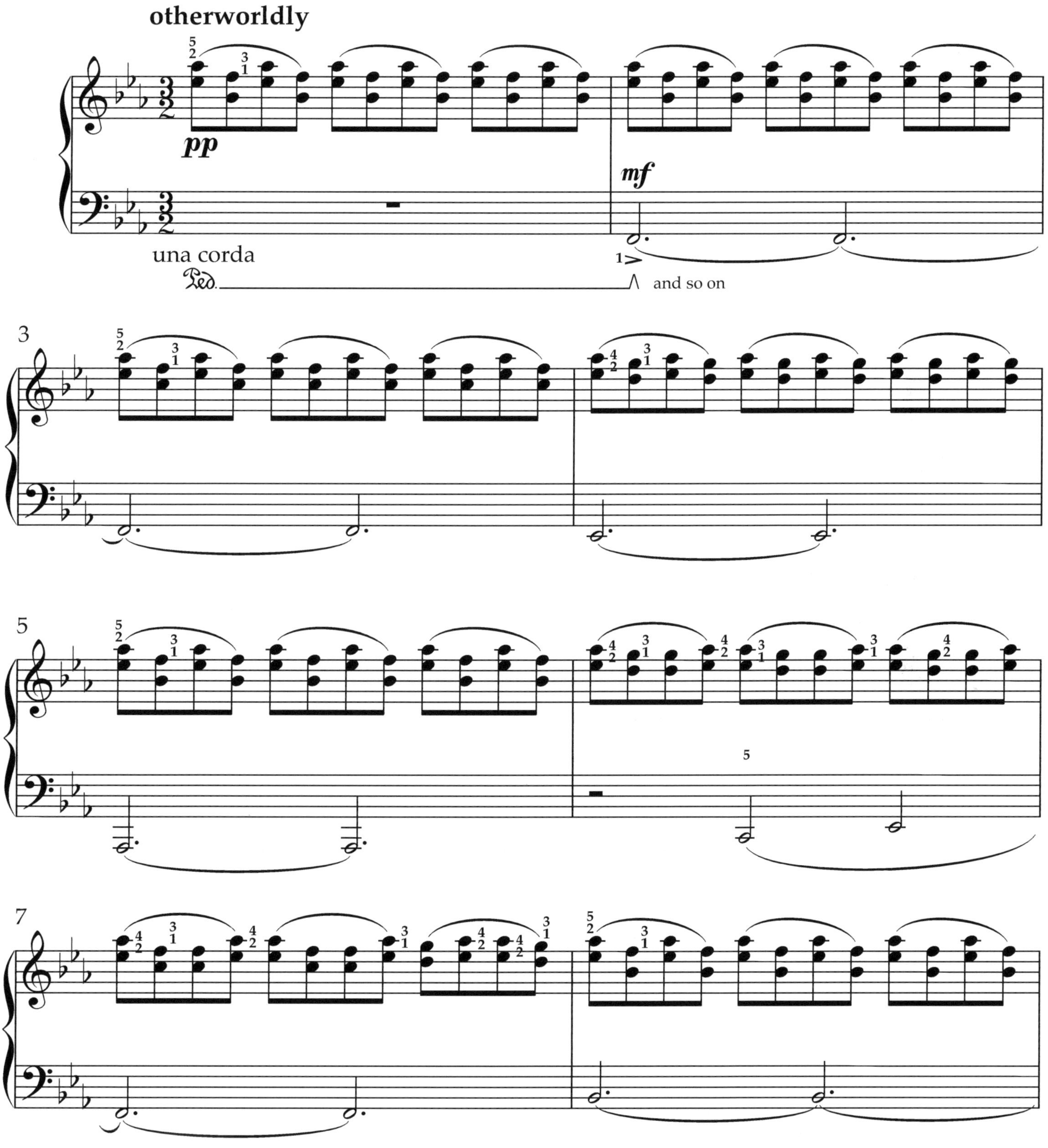

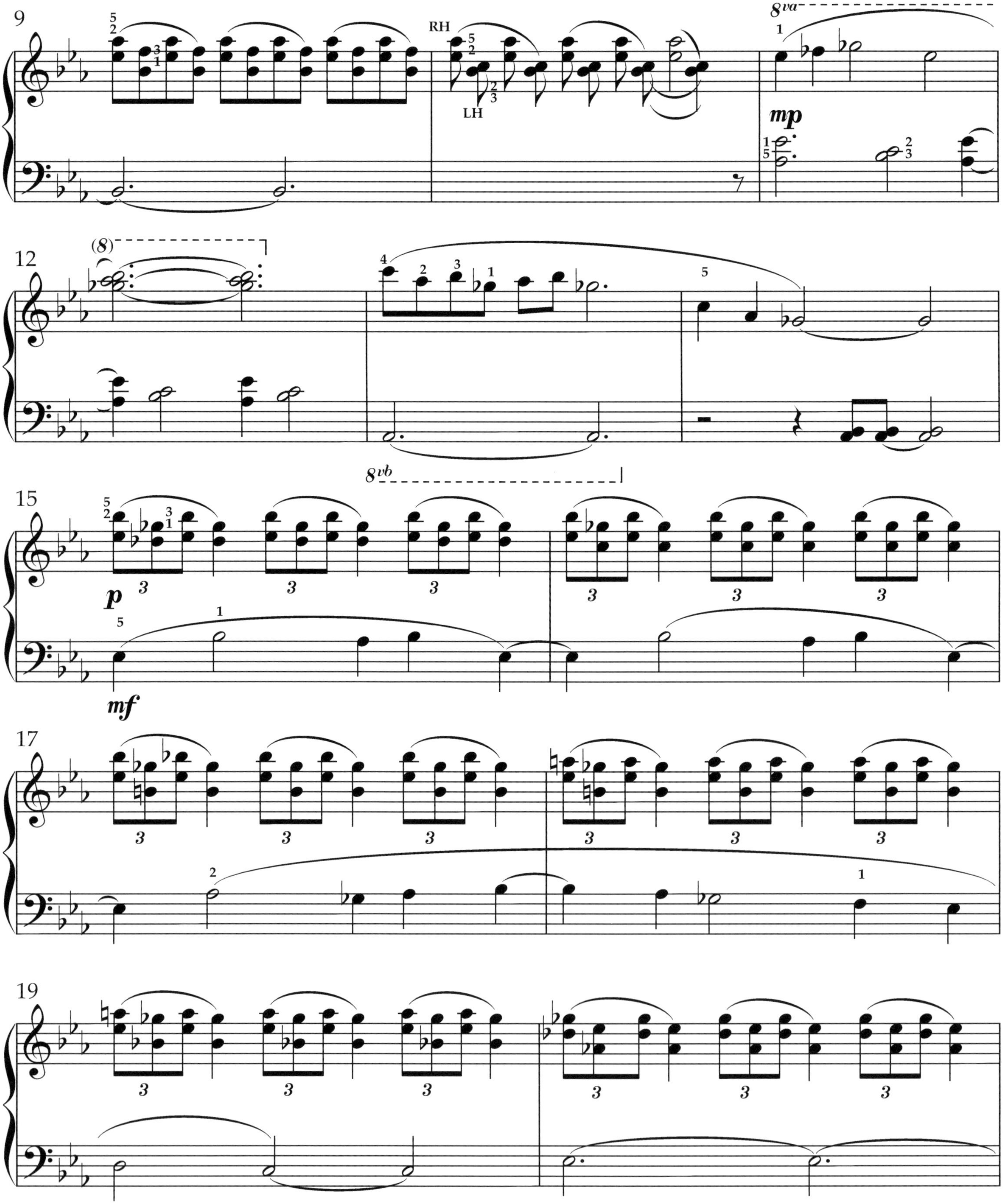
9
RH
LH
8va
mp
12
(8)
8vb
15
p
mf
17
19

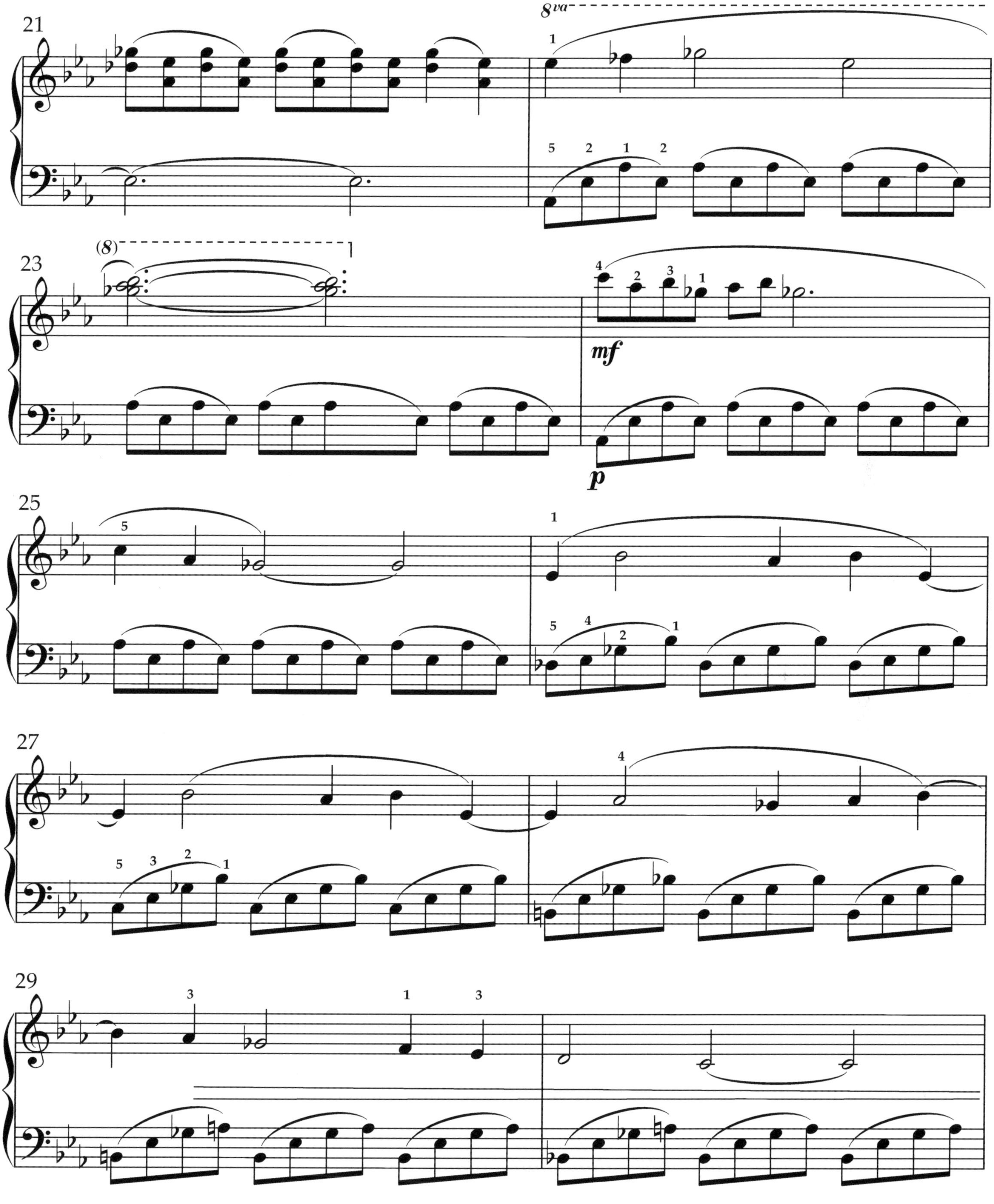
21
8va
23
(8)
mf
p
25
27
29

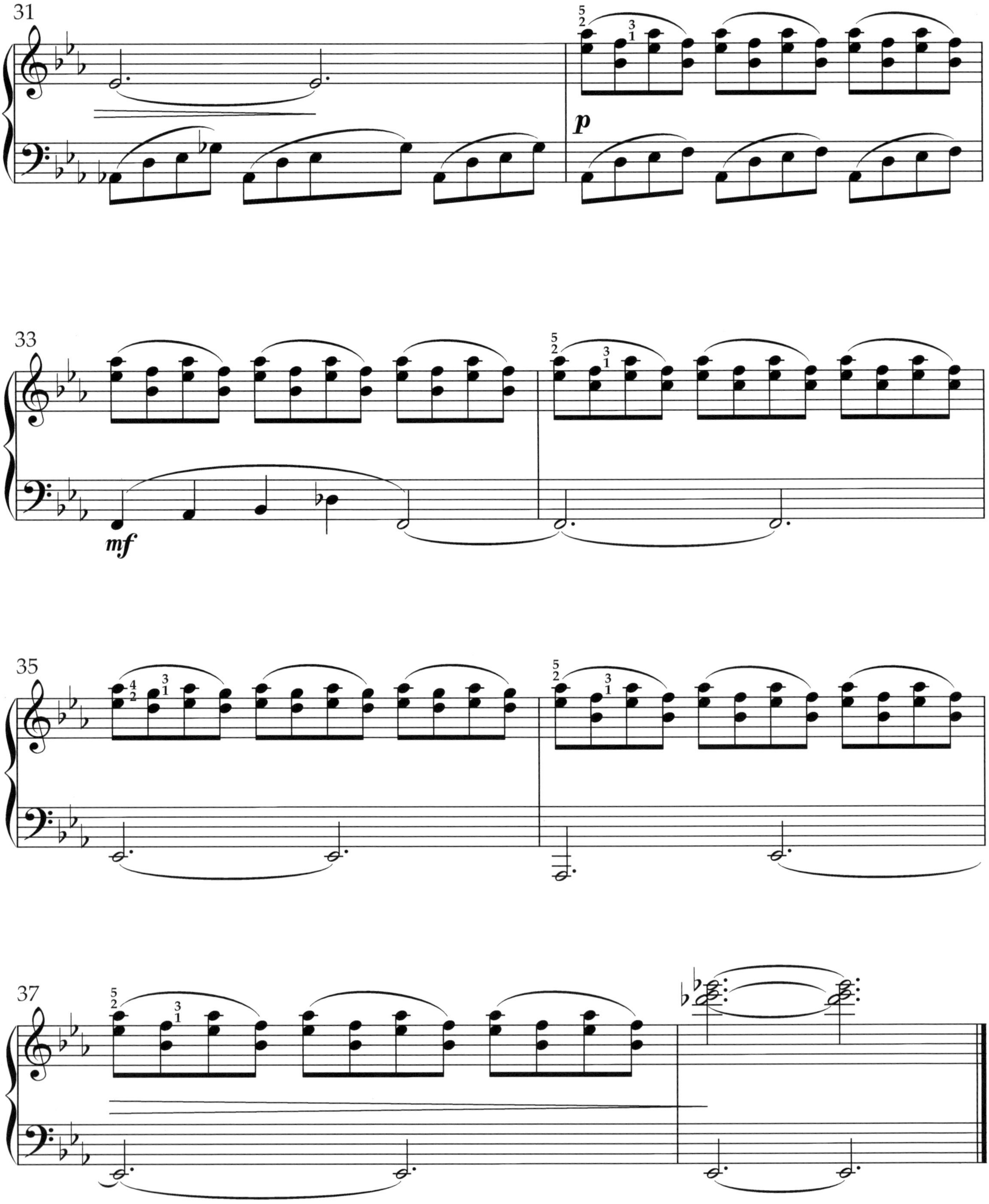
31
p
33
mf
35
37

Echoes of the Fallen

Elizabeth Bucura

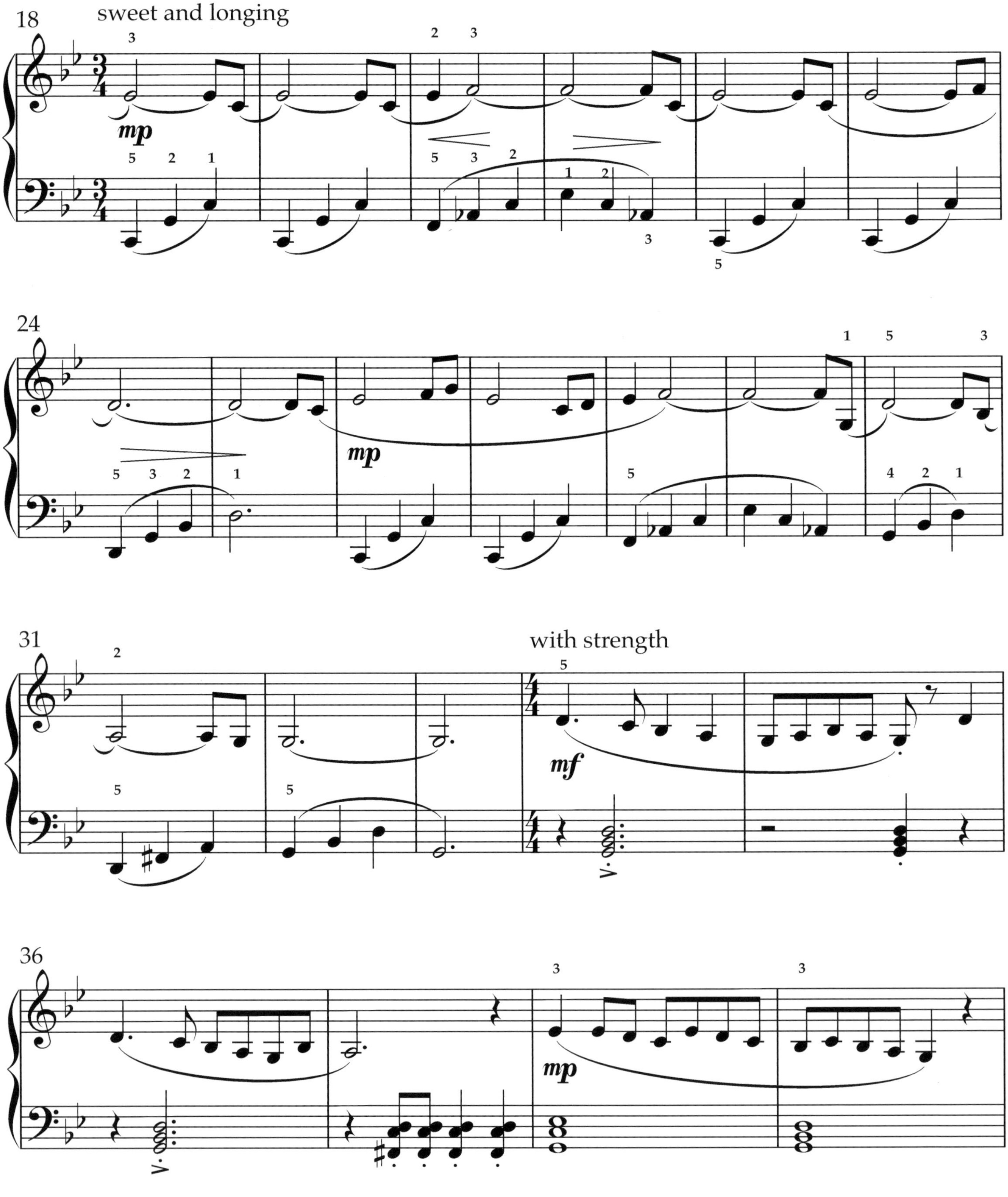
18
sweet and longing
mp
24
mp
31
with strength
mf
36
mp

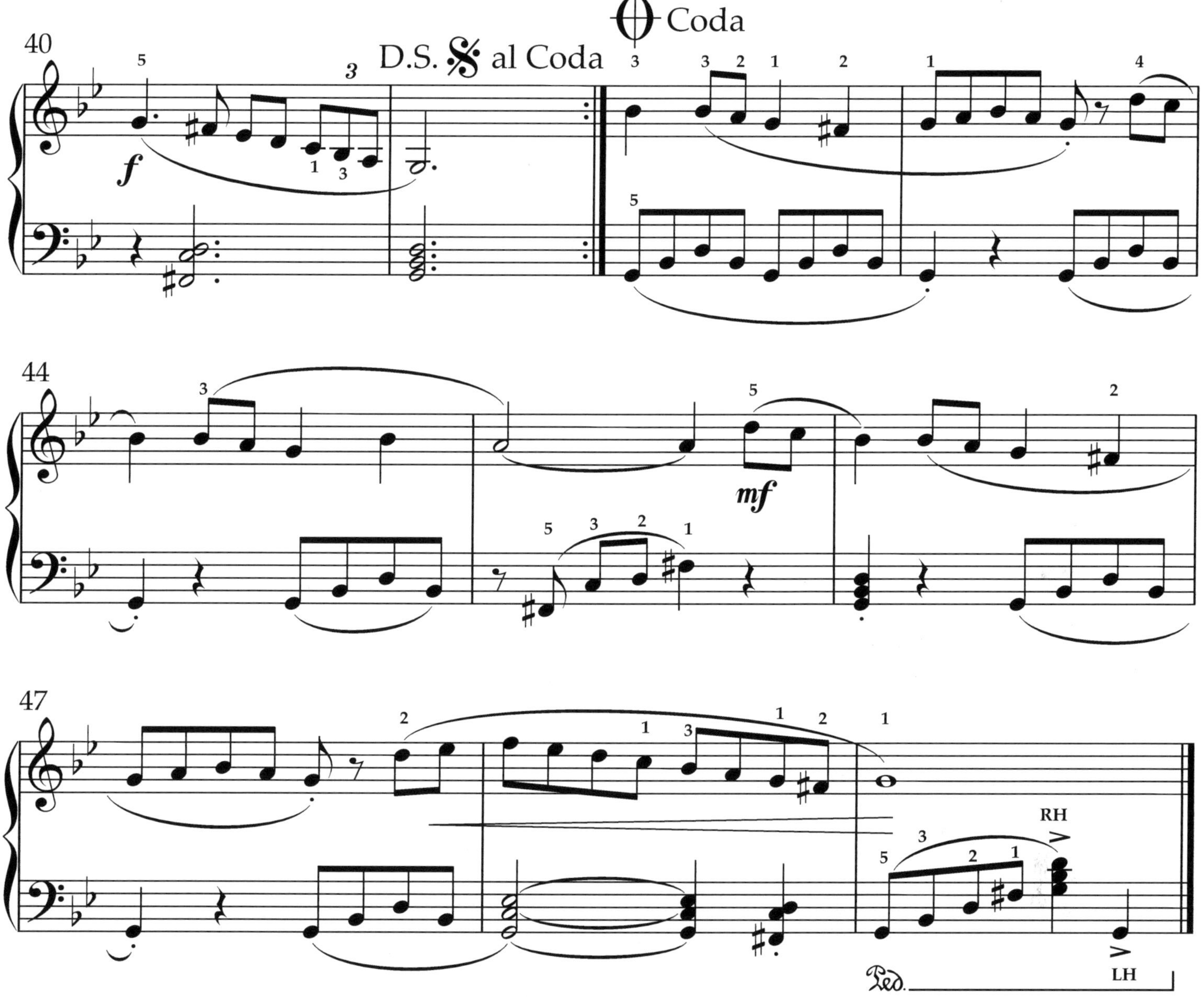

40
D.S. al Coda
Coda
f
44
mf
47
RH
LH
Ped.

Impish Reel

Elizabeth Bucura

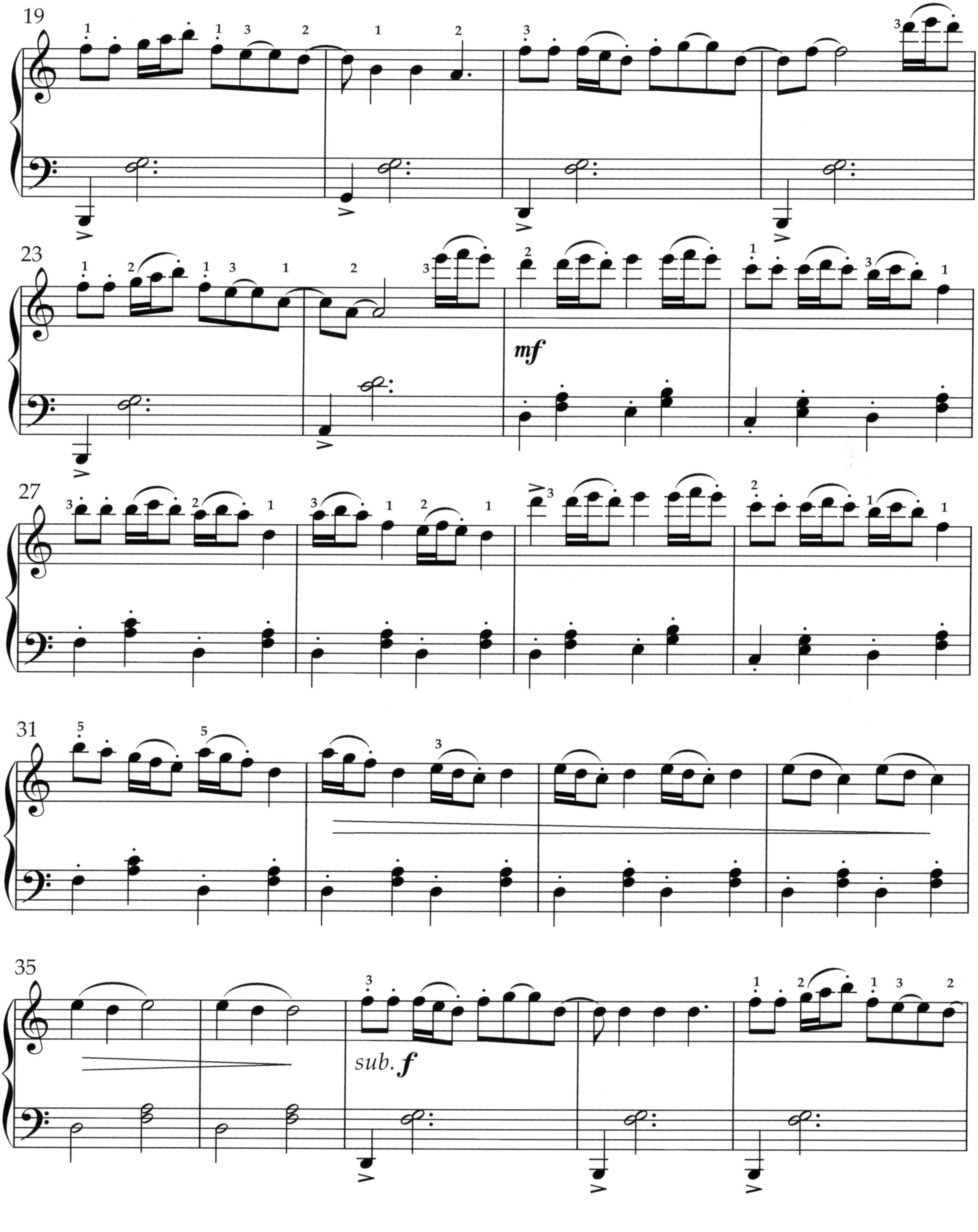
19
23
mf
27
31
35
sub. f

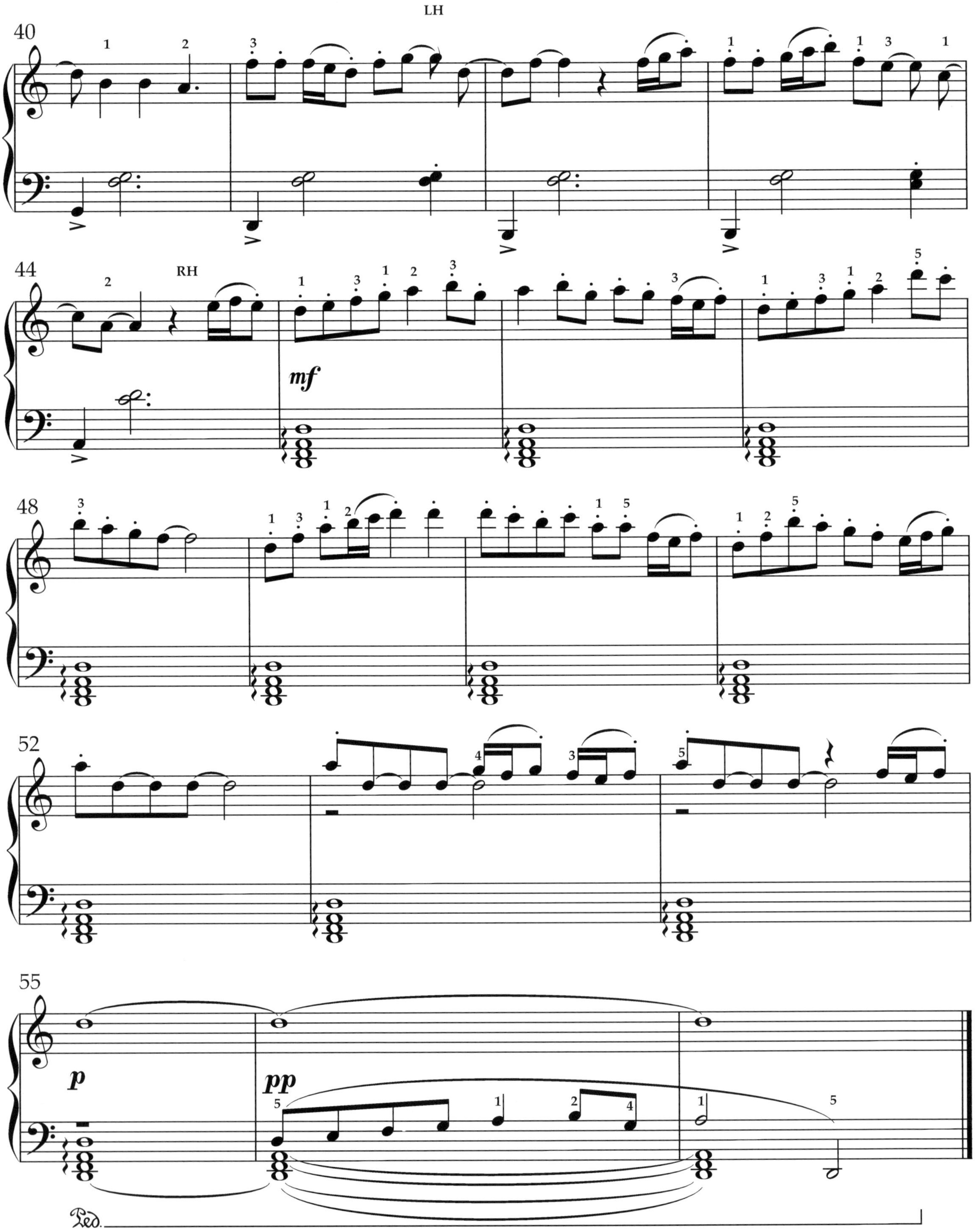
40
LH
44
RH
mf
48
52
55
p
pp
Ped.

Footpath of the Falling Sun

Elizabeth Bucura

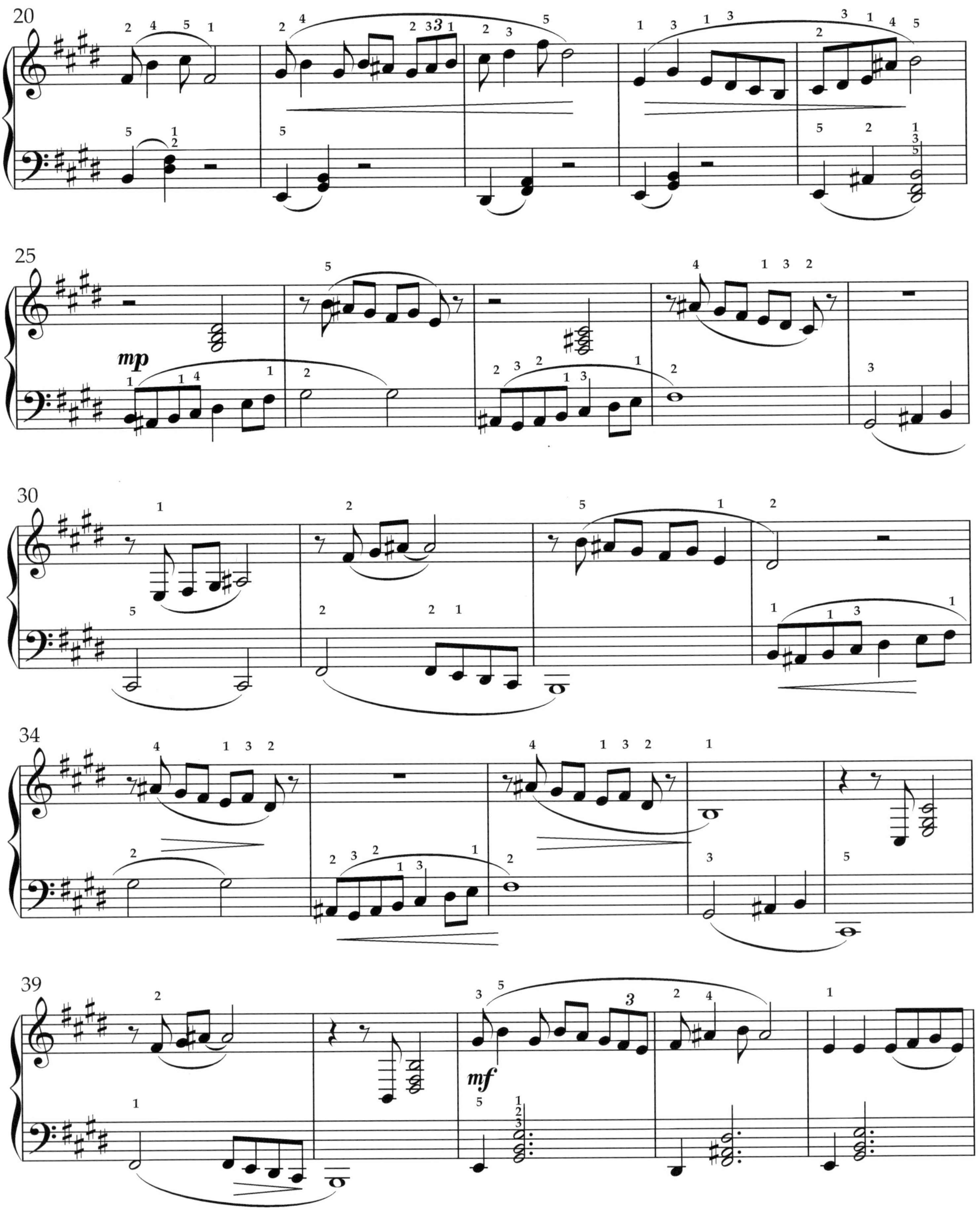
20
25
mp
30
34
39
mf

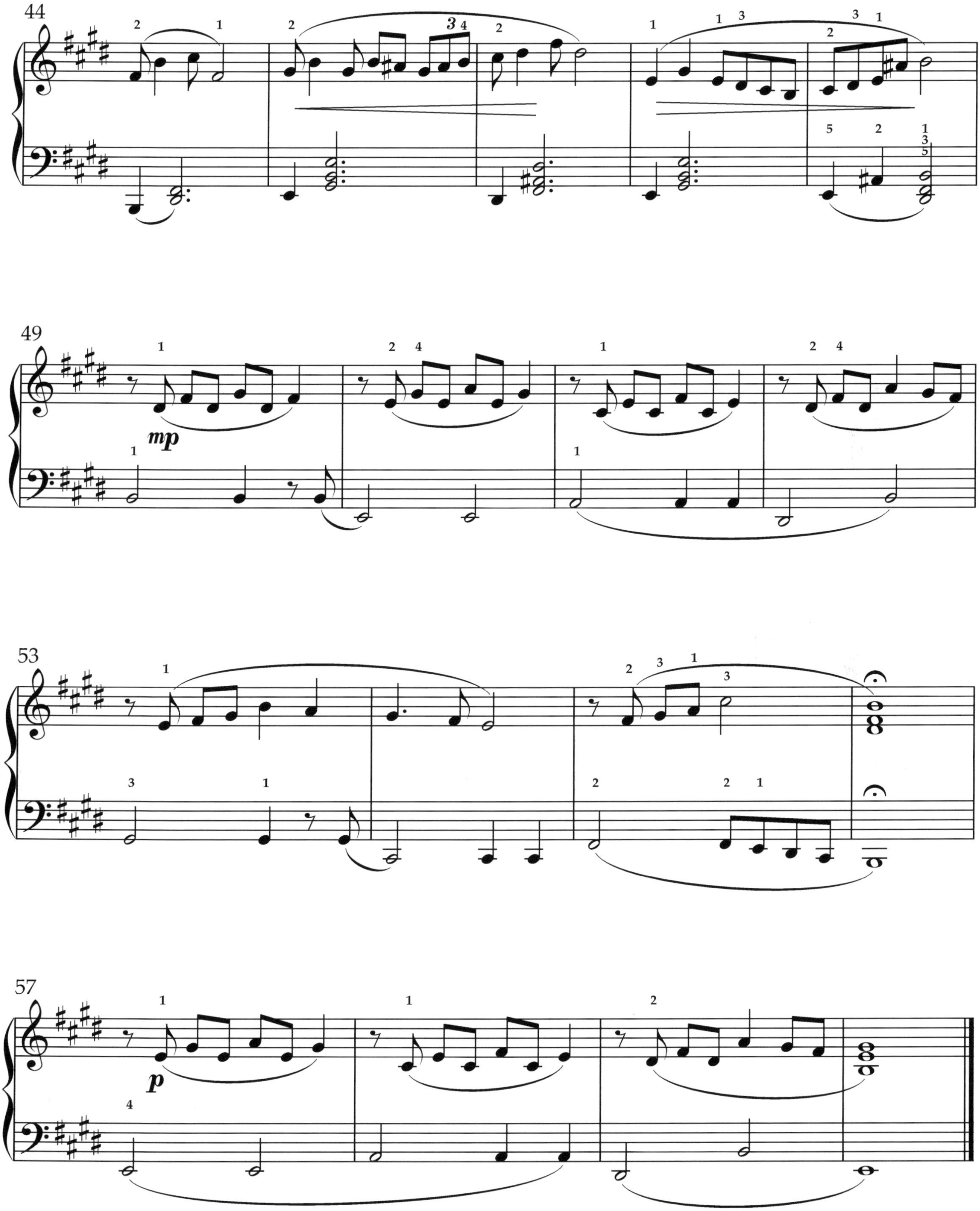
44
49
mp
53
57
p

Made in the USA
Coppell, TX
03 June 2025

50228325R00017